WHAT DOES AN EMT DO?

What Does a Community Helper Do?

Anna Louise Jordan

Words to Know

ambulance (AM-bu-lens)— A vehicle that carries sick or hurt people.

dispatcher (dis-PATCH-ur)— A person who answers a 911 call. The dispatcher tells EMTs, firefighters, and police officers where to go.

emergency (ee-MUR-jun-see)— Something that happens that needs quick action.

first aid (furst ayd)—Care that is given to a person before he or she is taken to a hospital.

first aid squad (furst ayd skwahd)—The people who are ready to help in an emergency.

technician (tek-NISH-un) — A person skilled in all parts of a job.

Enslow Elementary
an imprint of
Enslow Publishers, Inc.
40 Industrial Road   PO Box 38
Box 398   Aldershot
Berkeley Heights, NJ 07922   Hants GU12 6BP
USA   UK
http://www.enslow.com

Contents

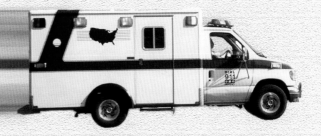

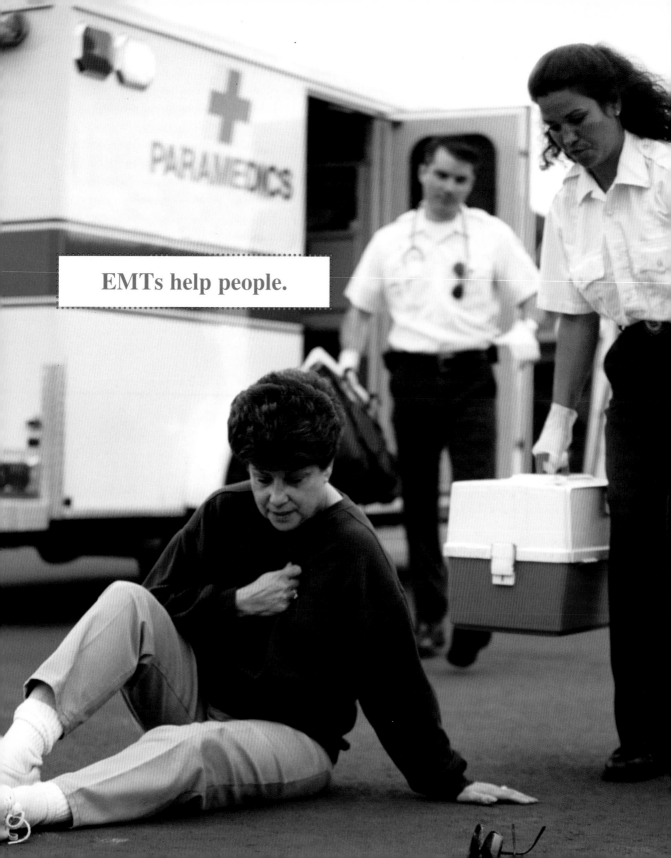

EMTs help people.

A Man Calls 911

A man calls 911. His wife has fallen, and her leg may be broken! The 911 dispatcher calls the first aid squad on a two-way radio. Soon an ambulance is on the way. There are three people on board. They are Emergency Medical Technicians, or EMTs for short.

When a person is hurt, EMTs come quickly.

EMTs and First Aid

EMTs know all about first aid. When there is an emergency, they come quickly. They help people who are sick. They help people who are hurt.

EMTs help people who are hurt. They help police officers and firefighters.

Do EMTs Work Alone?

EMTs are not doctors, but they work closely with emergency room doctors. They also work with police officers and firefighters.

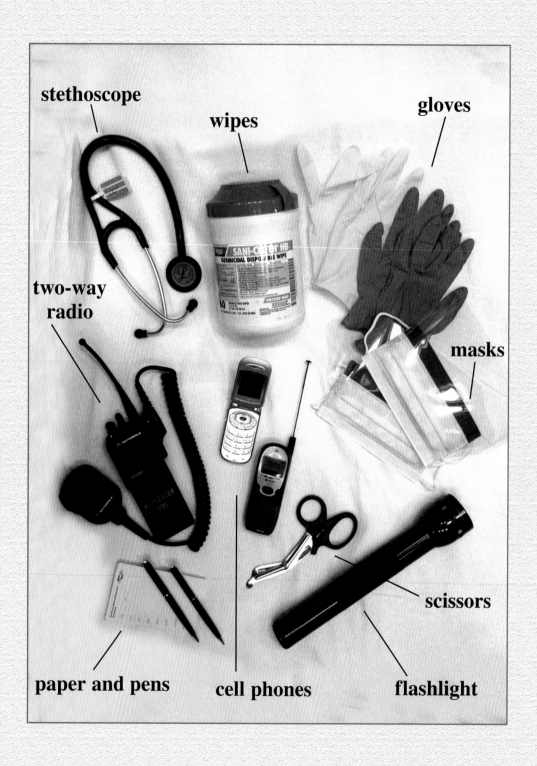

stethoscope

wipes

gloves

two-way radio

masks

paper and pens

cell phones

scissors

flashlight

What Do EMTs Wear?

Some EMTs wear uniforms. Some wear their own clothes. All of them carry tools to help in their work.

sheets and blankets

air tank

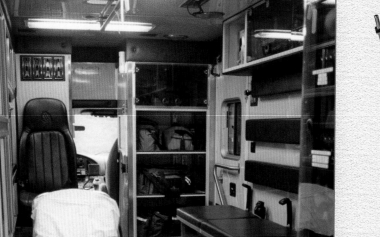

oxygen mask

first aid kit

stretcher

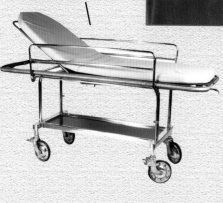

The inside of an ambulance can hold all the things EMTs need.

What Do EMTs Need?

The ambulance carries many more things the EMTs need:

- First aid kits
- Sheets and blankets
- Air tanks to help people breathe
- Stretchers for moving people safely

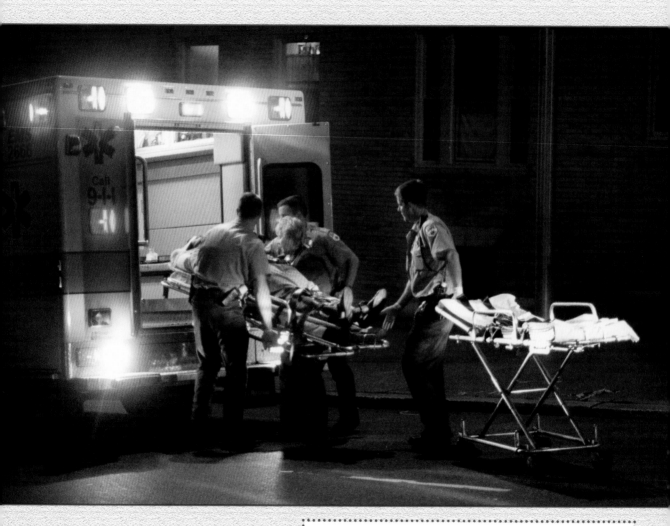

EMTs put people on stretchers.
The stretchers are put into
ambulances.

What Do EMTs Do?

Do you remember the woman who fell earlier in this book? She broke her leg. The EMTs put a splint on the woman's broken leg. They put her on a stretcher and lift her into the ambulance. Then they lock the stretcher to the wall. They are ready to drive the woman to the hospital.

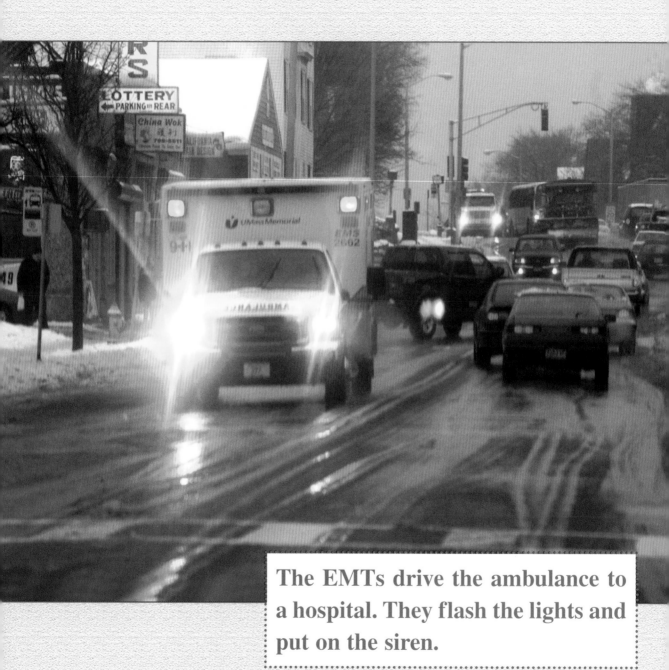

The EMTs drive the ambulance to a hospital. They flash the lights and put on the siren.

One of the EMTs drives the ambulance. She turns on the siren and honks the horn. She makes the lights flash. This tells other drivers, "Move out of the way! The ambulance is coming."

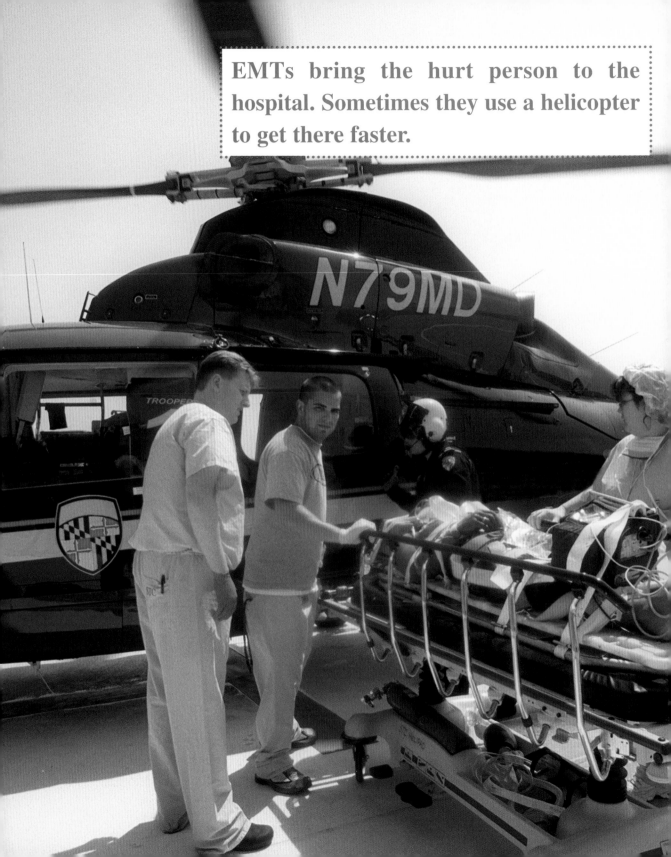

EMTs bring the hurt person to the hospital. Sometimes they use a helicopter to get there faster.

Another EMT talks to the hospital on the two-way radio. He tells the emergency room what kind of illness or injury the person has. The EMTs take the woman to the hospital. Doctors there take care of the woman's broken leg. The EMTs go back to their building to wait for the next call.

EMTs save lives and are community heroes.

EMTs Save Lives

Most EMTs work one day or one night a week. Most of them are volunteers. That means they do this job for free. They are EMTs because they want to help people. They want to save lives. EMTs are community heroes.

Helpful Phone Numbers

Make a list of helpful phone numbers to keep by the phone. You can make a list for each phone you have in your house. That way, if there is an emergency, you know who to call.

You will need (for one list):

- A lined piece of paper
- Pencil
- Crayons or stickers

1. On a lined piece of paper write down helpful phone numbers.
2. The first one should be 911.
3. Write your phone number and address.
4. Write the work phone numbers for the adults you live with.
5. Write the phone number of a family member that lives close by.
6. Write the phone number of a good neighbor you could go to for help.
7. You can draw pictures or put stickers on your list.
8. Place your list by the phone.

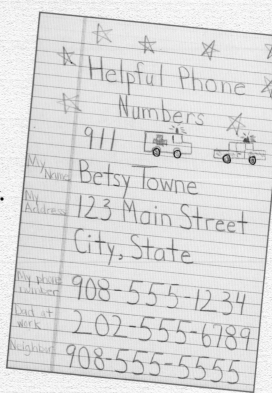

Learn More

Books

Gibson, Karen Bush. *Emergency Medical Technicians*. Mankato, Minn.: Bridgestone Books, 2001.

Hanson, Anne E. *Ambulances*. Mankato, Minn.: Bridgestone Books, 2001.

Levine, Michelle. *Ambulances*. Minneapolis, Minn.: Lerner Publications Co., 2004.

Internet Addresses

Kid's Space: For Kids Only
<http://legal.firn.edu/kids/kids.html>
This site has questions and answers that will help kids handle an emergency.

NIEHS On-line Coloring Pages
<http://www.niehs.nih.gov/kids/jvambul.htm>
Color an ambulance online or print it out.

Index

Note to Teachers and Parents: The *What Does a Community Helper Do?* series supports curriculum standards for K–4 learning about community services and helpers. The Words to Know section introduces subject-specific vocabulary. Early readers may require help with these new words.

Series Literacy Consultant:

Allan A. De Fina, Ph.D.
Past President of the New Jersey Reading Association
Professor, Department of Literacy Education
New Jersey City University

Enslow Elementary, an imprint of Enslow Publishers, Inc.

Enslow Elementary® is a registered trademark
of Enslow Publishers, Inc.

Library of Congress Cataloging-in-Publication Data

Jordan, Anna Louise.
    What does an EMT do? / Anna Louise Jordan.
        p. cm. — (What does a community helper do?)
    Includes bibliographical references and index.
    ISBN 0-7660-2540-3
    1. Emergency medical technicians—Juvenile literature. I.
Title. II. Series.
    RA645.5.J67 2004
    616.02'5'023—dc22
                            2004006891

Printed in the United States of America

10 9 8 7 6 5 4 3 2 1

To Our Readers:
We have done our best to make sure all Internet Addresses in this book were active and appropriate when we went to press. However, the author and the publisher have no control over and assume no liability for the material available on those Internet sites or on other Web sites they may link to. Any comments or suggestions can be sent by e-mail to comments@enslow.com or to the address on the back cover.

Illustration Credits: : COMSTOCK, p. 1; Enslow Publishers, Inc., p. 22; Hemera Technologies, Inc. 1997-2000, pp. 2, 3, 12 (objects around center photograph), 17, 19; Mark C. Ide, pp. 6, 8, 10, 12 (center), 14, 16, 18; PhotoDisc / Getty Images, pp. 4, 20.

Cover Illustration: COMSTOCK (bottom); top left to right, Mark C. Ide.